New England

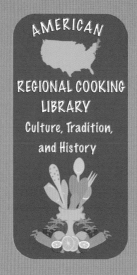

AMERICAN

REGIONAL COOKING
LIBRARY
Culture, Tradition,
and History

African American
American Indian
Amish and Mennonite
California
Hawaiian
Louisiana
Mexican American
Mid-Atlantic
Midwest
Northwest
New England
Southern
Southern Appalachia
Texas
Thanksgiving

New England

Mason Crest Publishers

Philadelphia

Mason Crest Publishers Inc.
370 Reed Road
Broomall, Pennsylvania 19008
(866) MCP-BOOK (toll free)
www.masoncrest.com

First printing
1 2 3 4 5 6 7 8 9 10

Library of Congress Cataloging-in-Publication Data

Libal, Joyce.
  New England / Joyce Libal.
     p. cm. — (American regional cooking library)
  Includes index.
  ISBN 1-59084-617-6
  1. Cookery, American—New England style—Juvenile literature. I. Title. II. Series.
  TX715.2.N48L52 2005
  641.5974—dc22
                              2004011080
Compiled by Joyce Libal.
Recipes by Patricia Therrien.
Recipes tested and prepared by Bonni Phelps.
Produced by Harding House Publishing Services, Inc., Vestal, New York.
Interior design by Dianne Hodack.
Cover design by Michelle Bouch.
Printed and bound in the Hashemite Kingdom of Jordan.

Contents

Introduction
by the Culinary Institute of America

Cooking is a dynamic profession, one that presents some of the greatest challenges and offers some of the greatest rewards. Since 1946, the Culinary Institute of America has provided aspiring and seasoned food service professionals with the knowledge and skills needed to become leaders and innovators in this industry.

Here at the CIA, we teach our students the fundamental culinary techniques they need to build a sound foundation for their food service careers. There is always another level of perfection for them to achieve and another skill to master. Our rigorous curriculum provides them with a springboard to continued growth and success.

Food is far more than simply sustenance or the source of energy to fuel you and your family through life's daily regimen. It conjures memories throughout life, summoning up the smell, taste, and flavor of simpler times. Cooking is more than an art and a science; it provides family history. Food prepared with care epitomizes the love, devotion, and culinary delights that you offer to your friends and family.

A cuisine provides a way to express and establish customs—the way a food should taste and the flavors and aromas associated with that food. Cuisines are more than just a collection of ingredients, cooking utensils, and dishes from a geographic location; they are elements that are critical to establishing a culinary identity.

When you can accurately read a recipe, you can trace a variety of influences by observing which ingredients are selected and also by noting the technique that is used. If you research the historical origins of a recipe, you may find ingredients that traveled from East to West or from the New World to the Old. Traditional methods of cooking a dish may have changed with the times or to meet special challenges.

The history of cooking illustrates the significance of innovation and the trading or sharing of ingredients and tools between societies. Although the various cooking vessels over the years have changed, the basic cooking methods have remained the same. Through adaptation, a recipe created years ago in a remote corner of the world could today be recognized by many throughout the globe.

When observing the customs of different societies, it becomes apparent that food brings people together. It is the common thread that we share and that we value. Regardless of the occasion, food is present to celebrate and to comfort. Through food we can experience other cultures and lands, learning the significance of particular ingredients and cooking techniques.

As you begin your journey through the culinary arts, keep in mind the power that food and cuisine holds. When passed from generation to generation, family heritage and traditions remain strong. Become familiar with the dishes your family has enjoyed through the years and play a role in keeping them alive. Don't be afraid to embellish recipes along the way – creativity is what cooking is all about.

New England Culture, History, and Traditions

Long ago, in 1620, the first English settlers landed on the northeastern coast of North America. Today, the states of Connecticut, Maine, Massachusetts, New Hampshire, Rhode Island, and Vermont are collectively known as New England. The area was named after the colonists' old home. They had brought many English customs and traditions with them, but their new home was still a new world for them.

Those early settlers had a lot to learn from American Indians who were already living in the area. The Wampanoag Indians taught the English colonists about crops that were suited to the short growing season and methods for farming the rocky soil. Without the Natives' help, the Pilgrims would probably not have survived their first winter.

The simple foods made by American Indians played a significant role in the food traditions that developed in New England. Immigrant cooks were able to learn from the American Indians and incorporate knowledge they brought with them from Europe into a cuisine based on flavorful foods available in the area.

The ocean was an important source of food in New England. So bountiful was the Atlantic coast that Pilgrims sent letters home praising the ease of obtaining various types of seafood by simply lowering a net into the water. Shellfish such as lobster and clams, as well as cod, haddock, flounder, and bass were all abundant. Farther inland, wild meat like venison and bear and wild fowl such as turkey, pheasants, and geese were plentiful.

Over the years, immigrants from many lands including Italy, Ireland and Eastern Europe have moved to New England, yet it retains the strong cooking heritage of the first settlers. Yorkshire puddings and London broil are examples of the cooking heritage the English settlers brought with them and incorporated into a New England cuisine that is characterized by simplicity in terms of preparation and hearty flavors from a mix of basic ingredients. This honest, good-tasting food can be broadly characterized as "comfort food," as it is filling and satisfying—perfect food for the long, cold winters that are common in New England.

Before you cook...

If you haven't done much cooking before, you may find recipe books a little confusing. Certain words and terms can seem unfamiliar. You may find the measurements difficult to understand. What appears to be an easy or familiar dish may contain ingredients you've never heard of before. You might not understand what utensil the recipe calls for you to use, or you might not be sure what the recipe is asking you to do.

Reading the pages in this section before you get started may help you understand the directions better so that your cooking goes more smoothly. You can also refer back to these pages whenever you run into questions.

Safety Tips

Cooking involves handling very hot and very sharp objects, so being careful is common sense. What's more, you want to be certain that anything you plan on putting in your mouth is safe to eat. If you follow these easy tips, you should find that cooking can be both fun and safe.

Before you cook...

- Always wash your hands before and after handling food. This is particularly important after you handle raw meats, poultry, and eggs, as bacteria called salmonella can live on these uncooked foods. You can't see or smell salmonella, but these germs can make you or anyone who swallows them very sick.
- Make a habit of using potholders or oven mitts whenever you handle pots and pans from the oven or microwave.
- Always set pots, pans, and knives with their handles away from counter edges. This way you won't risk catching your sleeves on them—and any younger children in the house won't be in danger of grabbing something hot or sharp.
- Don't leave perishable food sitting out of the refrigerator for more than an hour or two.
- Wash all raw fruits and vegetables to remove dirt and chemicals.
- Use a cutting board when chopping vegetables or fruit, and always cut away from yourself.
- Don't overheat grease or oil—but if grease or oil does catch fire, don't try to extinguish the flames with water. Instead, throw baking soda or salt on the fire to put it out. Turn all stove burners off.
- If you burn yourself, immediately put the burn under cold water, as this will prevent the burn from becoming more painful.
- Never put metal dishes or utensils in the microwave. Use only microwave-proof dishes.
- Wash cutting boards and knives thoroughly after cutting meat, fish or poultry — especially when raw and before using the same tools to prepare other foods such as vegetables and cheese. This will prevent the spread of bacteria such as salmonella.
- Keep your hands away from any moving parts of appliances, such as mixers.
- Unplug any appliance, such as a mixer, blender, or food processor before assembling for use or disassembling after use.

Metric Conversion Table

Most cooks in the United States use measuring containers based on an eight-ounce cup, a teaspoon, and a tablespoon. Meanwhile, cooks in Canada and Europe are more apt to use metric measurements. The recipes in this book use cups, teaspoons, and tablespoons—but you can convert these measurements to metric by using the table below.

Temperature
To convert Fahrenheit degrees to Celsius, subtract 32 and multiply by .56.

212°F = 100°C
(this is the boiling point of water)
250°F = 110°C
275°F = 135°C
300°F = 150°C
325°F = 160°C
350°F = 180°C
375°F = 190°C
400°F = 200°C

Liquid Measurements
1 teaspoon = 5 milliliters
1 tablespoon = 15 milliliters
1 fluid ounce = 30 milliliters
1 cup = 240 milliliters
1 pint = 480 milliliters
1 quart = 0.95 liters
1 gallon = 3.8 liters

Measurements of Mass or Weight
1 ounce = 28 grams
8 ounces = 227 grams
1 pound (16 ounces) = 0.45 kilograms
2.2 pounds = 1 kilogram

Measurements of Length
¼ inch = 0.6 centimeters
½ inch = 1.25 centimeters
1 inch = 2.5 centimeters

Pan Sizes

Baking pans are usually made in standard sizes. The pans used in the United States are roughly equivalent to the following metric pans:

9-inch cake pan = 23-centimeter pan
11x7-inch baking pan = 28x18-centimeter baking pan
13x9-inch baking pan = 32.5x23-centimeter baking pan
9x5-inch loaf pan = 23x13-centimeter loaf pan
2-quart casserole = 2-liter casserole

Useful Tools, Utensils, Dishes

blender

candy thermometer

cheese grater

slow cooker

double boiler

electric mixer

flour sifter

garlic press

ice cream scoop

loaf pan

nut chopper

stock pot

pancake griddle

pastry blender

pie plate

rolling pin

waffle iron

wire whisk

Cooking Glossary

cut Mix solid shortening or butter into flour, usually by using a pastry blender or two knives and making short, chopping strokes until the mixture looks like small pellets.

dash A very small amount, just a couple of drops or shakes.

diced Cut into small cubes or pieces.

dollop A small mound, about 1 or 2 tablespoons.

dot To take a small amount of a substance (usually butter), divide it into small pieces, and evenly distribute the pieces over the surface of food.

fold Gently combine a lighter substance with a heavier batter by spooning the lighter mixture through the heavier one without using strong beating strokes.

minced Cut into very small pieces.

score To cut narrow slashes across the surface of a food.

set When a food preparation has completed the thickening process and can be sliced.

simmer Gently boiling, so that the surface of the liquid just ripples.

toss Turn food over quickly and lightly so that it is evenly covered with a liquid or powder.

whisk Stir briskly with a wire whisk.

zest A piece of the peel of lemon, lime, or orange that has been grated.

New England Flavors

apples

blueberries

cinnamon

cloves

cranberries

ginger

maple syrup

molasses

walnuts

New England Recipes

New England Food History

American Indians had many uses for blueberries, which they generously shared with the pilgrims. Drying blueberries in the sun was a way to preserve them for use during all seasons of the year. Sometimes they were ground into a sort of blueberry flour. One sophisticated use for this product was as a dry rub to season meat before cooking. Another tasty way to use it was in a pudding that the Indians called *sautauthig*. Wild blueberries and cranberries were abundant during colonial times and are among the commercial crops grown in New England today.

Blueberry Waffles

Ingredients:

2 cups flour
½ teaspoon salt
2 tablespoons sugar
4 teaspoons baking powder
2 eggs
1½ cups yogurt
¼ cup butter, melted
1 cup blueberries, fresh or frozen

Cooking utensils you'll need:
measuring cups
measuring spoons
2 mixing bowls
flour sifter
wire whisk
waffle iron

Directions:

Lightly grease and preheat the waffle iron. Sift the flour, salt, sugar, and baking powder into one bowl. *Whisk* the eggs and yogurt in the second bowl. Stir the egg mixture into the flour mixture, and stir in the melted butter. Fold in blueberries. Pour about ½ cup of the mixture onto the waffle iron, close the lid, and cook until done. (Cooking time can vary between different waffle irons.) Do not lift the lid until done, but be cautious to not overbake. Carefully lift the waffle from the iron, and serve with maple syrup.

Johnny Cakes

Maple syrup is the perfect accompaniment for these traditional cornmeal pancakes that have been made since at least the 1700s.

Ingredients:

1 cup cornmeal
½ teaspoon salt
1 teaspoon sugar
water
milk

Cooking utensils you'll need:
measuring cup
measuring spoons
saucepan or teakettle
mixing bowl
pancake griddle

Directions:

Put about 1 cup of water in the saucepan or teakettle, and bring it to a boil. Stir together the cornmeal, salt, and sugar in the bowl. Slowly stir in just enough boiling water to make the mixture "swell," and set it aside for 5 minutes. Lightly grease and preheat the pancake griddle. Stir just enough milk into the mixture to make it thin enough to easily drop from a spoon. Use a ¼-cup measure to pour the mixture onto the hot griddle. Cook each side of the johnny cakes until well browned, and serve hot with a pat of cold butter and maple syrup. Shown here served with sour cream and salsa with green onion.

New England Food History

Since its founding by a clergyman seeking religious freedom from the Puritans in Massachusetts, Rhode Island, the "ocean state," has been known for freedom of religious choice. It is also famous for its johnny cake. According to legend, clergyman Roger Williams, the founder of Providence Plantation, Rhode Island's first permanent settlement, was actually the first settler who learned to make johnny cakes.

Traditional johnny cakes are made using whitecap flint corn. The name "flint" is used because the corn is particularly hard; when ground, it produces a meal that is not as fine as regular cornmeal. This is the type of corn originally used by the Narragansett Indians, who cooked their pancakes on hot rocks. The Narragansett are the ones who taught the first European colonists how to make johnny cake.

Whitecap flint corn grows well in Rhode Island, and it used to be cultivated throughout the state. The fact that it produces a low yield per plant and is difficult to grind, however, has made it a less popular crop today.

Some people think the name johnny cake comes from "journey cake," a name given to this food because it was durable enough to be taken on long trips. Others think that trappers who learned to make the cakes from Shawnee Indians originally called the pancakes "Shawneecakes," a term that sounds a bit like johnny cakes. Over the years, the original term may have been altered to produce the name that is familiar today.

Hot Mulled Cider

"Mulled" is a term used for a hot beverage that contains spices.

Ingredients:

½ gallon apple cider
¼ cup maple syrup
¼ cup brown sugar
3 cinnamon sticks
½ teaspoon whole cloves

Cooking utensils you'll need:
measuring cups
measuring spoon
large kettle
strainer

Directions:

Stir together the apple cider, maple syrup, and brown sugar in the kettle. Add the cinnamon sticks and whole cloves, and bring mixture to a boil. Immediately reduce heat, and *simmer* for 5 to 10 minutes. Strain and pour the hot cider into mugs.

Tips:

Garnish each serving with a fresh cinnamon stick if desired.

For a low-calorie alternative, eliminate maple syrup and brown sugar.

New England Food History

Before the days of refrigeration, which preserves fresh cider, the word "cider" meant fermented apple juice (apple juice with alcohol in it). Time and natural yeast occurring in the juice from pressed apples were all that was needed to produce this drink that was popular with the Pilgrims and other settlers. Today the term "hard cider" is used for cider that contains alcohol.

Apples are not native to North America. We have the first settlers to thank for carrying apple seeds from Europe and planting them here.

Boston Brown Bread

Traditional Boston Brown Bread is steamed, but this easy recipe lets you pop it in the oven.

Preheat oven to 350° Fahrenheit.

Ingredients:

2 cups whole wheat flour
1 cup white flour
2 teaspoons baking soda
½ teaspoon salt
2 cups buttermilk
¼ cup molasses
⅔ cup brown sugar, firmly packed
¾ cup chopped walnuts
1 cup raisins

Cooking utensils you'll need:
measuring cups
measuring spoons
2 mixing bowls
nut chopper
loaf pan (see "Tips")
baking rack

Directions:

Grease and lightly flour the loaf pan and set it aside. Mix together the flours, baking soda, and salt in one mixing bowl. Mix the buttermilk, molasses, and brown sugar in the second bowl. Stir the wet ingredients into the dry ingredients, and *fold* in chopped nuts and raisins. Pour into the prepared loaf pan, and bake for 60 minutes. Cool in pan on baking rack for about 5 minutes before removing loaf from pan. Do not slice until completely cooled.

Tips:

Traditional Boston Brown Bread is round. To make pretty round loaves, simply bake the bread in one-pound coffee cans instead of a loaf pan. Make sure the top of each can is smooth so you don't cut your hand when greasing the cans. Only fill the cans ½ to ⅔ full so the bread has room to rise as it bakes. If you have trouble removing the baked bread from a can, use a can opener to cut the bottom off the can, and push the bread out of the cylinder.

To test cakes and cake-like breads for doneness, insert a wooden toothpick into the cake or bread. If there are no crumbs on the toothpick when you remove it, the item is done.

New England Food History

Molasses was a favorite early New England ingredient, but Columbus is the one credited with bringing molasses to the "New World." Eventually, it became the most prevalent sweetener in colonial America. Candies that were made with this sweetener in England were called toffee. In North America, this evolved to "taffy," and "pulling taffy" became a fun activity that people enjoyed.

Molasses was also an important ingredient in rum, an alcoholic beverage enjoyed by men, women, and children in the English colonies. The Molasses Act of 1733 angered colonists by placing a heavy tax on molasses originating anywhere other than British Islands in the Caribbean. This tension was one of the causes of the Revolutionary War.

Unfortunately, molasses also played an important role in the slave trade. It was produced by slaves in the Caribbean, shipped to North America where much of it was made into rum, then shipped to West Africa, where it was used to purchase slaves who were sent to the Caribbean. There, they were traded for molasses to ship to northern shores. Slaves were also brought to colonies in the South and in New England. This molasses–rum–slaves commerce is sometimes referred to as the triangular trade.

Molasses lost much of its popularity after World War I, when the price of cane sugar fell.

Vermont Cheddar/Vegetable Soup

Preheat oven to 425 degrees Fahrenheit.

Ingredients:

1½ tablespoons butter
½ cup **minced** onion
⅓ cup minced celery
⅓ cup minced carrot
½ teaspoon caraway seeds (optional)
3 tablespoons flour
⅓ cup white cooking wine
1½ cups chicken broth (Use more to thin soup as desired.)
¾ teaspoon Worcestershire sauce
1½ cups chopped cauliflower
1¼ cups grated extra-sharp cheddar cheese
dash of Tabasco sauce (optional)
salt and pepper to taste

Cooking utensils you'll need:
measuring cups
measuring spoons
cheese grater
large saucepan

Directions:

Melt butter in saucepan over medium heat. Stir in minced onion, celery, carrots, and caraway seeds. Cook and stir until onions are translucent. Stir in flour and continue cooking, stirring constantly, until flour is lightly browned (about 3 minutes). Stir in wine and bring to boil. Immediately add chicken broth, Worcestershire sauce, and cauliflower. Return to boil, lower heat, cover, and *simmer* until cauliflower is tender (about 15 minutes). Add cheese, and stir until melted. Stir in additional chicken broth if the soup is too thick. Add a dash of Tabasco sauce, if desired, and salt and pepper to taste.

Continue cooking until heated through, and serve hot.

Tips:

Alcohol evaporates from wine when it is boiled, leaving the flavor behind.

New England Food History

Dairy cows arrived in New England in the seventeenth century along with the first settlers. Colonists also brought the equipment and knowledge necessary to make cheese. By the middle of the nineteenth century, milk was being shipped to other parts of the country via the railroad. Today, New England has a reputation for producing high-quality cheese.

Vermont was first explored by Samuel de Champlain, a French explorer, and it was named for the green mountains that roll across its surface. (*Vert* is the French word for green and *mont* is French for mountain.) After 1760, many settlers from Massachusetts and Connecticut moved to this area.

New England Clam Chowder

There are countless recipes for chowder. The first known written recipe for this thick or thin fish stew dates to the mid-1800s. The recipe below is newer and uses several readily available herbs and vegetables.

Ingredients:

3 tablespoons olive oil
½ teaspoon **minced** garlic
1 cup **diced** onions
1 cup diced celery
1 cup diced carrots
¾ gallon clam stock or juice
½ teaspoon salt
1 teaspoon thyme
½ teaspoon basil
½ teaspoon oregano
3 large potatoes, peeled and diced
2 cups drained, chopped clams
¾ cup butter
¾ cup flour

Cooking utensils you'll need:
measuring cups
measuring spoons
stockpot
skillet

Directions:

Place oil in stockpot over medium heat. Add garlic, onion, celery, and carrots, and cook, stirring occasionally, until vegetables are tender (about 10 minutes). Stir in clam stock, salt, herbs, and potatoes, and bring to a boil. Meanwhile, melt butter in the skillet over medium heat, add flour, and cook, stirring constantly, until flour is lightly browned. Add browned flour to chowder, reduce heat, and *simmer* for about 1 hour. Serve hot.

New England Food History

Where did the word "chowder" come from? In the old days, fishermen in France often cooked potluck fish stew in a three-legged pot called a *chaudiere*. Many people think this may be the origin of the word "chowder." Other people think it might be a corruption of the word "jowter," an English word for someone who sells fish. Whatever the origin of the word "chowder," it is believed that American Indians, specifically members of the Micmac tribe, may have been the first people in the New World to cook and eat this now-world-famous soup.

Many different types of fish and vegetables can be used to make chowder. Cod may have been the first fish used to make this flavorful soup. In some areas of the country, clam chowder is made with tomatoes. People in New England are usually opposed to this ingredient in chowder. In fact, a bill was introduced into the Maine State Legislature in 1939 to make adding tomatoes to chowder a "statutory and culinary offense."

New England Food History

Cranberries were growing wild in America long before the arrival of the first European settlers, and American Indians were the first to use this food. Today, Massachusetts is one of the top producers of these nutritious berries.

The first person known to cultivate cranberries for commercial use was a man named Henry Hall, who did so in the early nineteenth century. This Massachusetts farmer developed a technique for growing cranberries that is still used today. It is called "sand layering" and involves placing a layer of sand over acid peat soil. That and fresh water are all that is needed to grow this crop that was a popular food stored on ships in the 1800s. The fruit's high vitamin C content and ability to last for long periods of time were useful in preventing scurvy, a disease that affected sailors who spent much time at sea.

New England Cranberry Sauce

This native American fruit was served in 1621 at the first Thanksgiving. Today, it is a healthy addition to the menu any time of the year.

Ingredients:

1 cup water
2 cups sugar
2 cups cranberries (fresh or frozen)
dash of cinnamon or cloves
1 teaspoon lemon or orange **zest**

Cooking utensils you'll need:
measuring cups
measuring spoon
saucepan

Directions:

Stir sugar into water in saucepan, and add remaining ingredients. Place over medium heat, and boil gently until berries burst. Continue simmering until liquid is reduced as desired, remembering that the sauce will continue to thicken as it cools. Pour into a serving dish, and refrigerate to chill before serving.

Maple-Sweetened Acorn Squash

Preheat oven to 350° Fahrenheit.

Ingredients:

2 medium acorn squash
1 slice bacon
½ teaspoon cinnamon
⅛ teaspoon cloves
2 tablespoons butter
¼ cup plus 2 tablespoons maple syrup
¼ teaspoon nutmeg
¼ teaspoon salt

Cooking utensils you'll need:
measuring cup
measuring spoons
small mixing bowl
small saucepan or teakettle
baking dish

Directions:

Wash and cut each squash in half in the same direction as the ribs grow. Scoop out and discard seeds. Cut a small sliver off the center of the uncut side of each squash to make it flat enough to stand (cut side up) in the baking dish. Cut bacon into 4 pieces and set them aside. Bring a couple cups of water to a boil in the saucepan or teakettle. Mix remaining ingredients together in the bowl, and place an equal amount of the mixture in the cavity of each squash. Top each with a piece of bacon, pour about ½ to 1 inch of water in the baking dish, and bake for 1 hour.

New England Food History

Askutasquash is the Indian word that was used in Massachusetts for squash, a vegetable that ranked with corn and beans as one of the most important foods cultivated by American Indians prior to the arrival of Europeans. When the Spanish conquistadors first arrived in South America, winter squash was already being grown there. Some types of squash are also native to Central America and Mexico. In fact, squash or pumpkin seeds dating before 4000 B.C. have been found during archeological digs in Mexico. American Indians ate both the seeds and flowers of this plant, as well as the meaty portion of the vegetable.

New England History

It's not only New England's food that's important to the United States! From the time of the Mayflower Compact, which established a democratic government at Plymouth Rock, to the Boston Tea Party that helped ignite the Revolutionary War, New England has been important to the nation's politics, culture, and philosophy. It is credited with the birth of the "town meeting," still an important part of local politics. Many of the nation's most famous leaders, including John Adams, John Quincy Adams, Clara Barton, Calvin Coolidge, Benjamin Franklin, Nathan Hale, Franklin Pierce, Paul Revere, Margaret Chase Smith, and Daniel Webster, were from New England.

Harvard Beets

Founded in 1636, Harvard is the nation's first college. A Yale version of this dish is also popular. In that case, lemon juice and orange juice are used in place of the vinegar. Cooked either way, beets are great for adding bright color and taste to the dinner menu

Ingredients:

6 medium-sized raw beets (or two 16-ounce cans)
½ cup white or cider vinegar
½ cup sugar
1 tablespoon flour
¼ teaspoon salt
2 tablespoons butter

Cooking utensils you'll need:
measuring cups
measuring spoons
vegetable scrub brush
saucepan

Directions:

Scrub beets well, place them in saucepan, add water to cover, place over medium heat, bring to boil, cover, and *simmer* until tender (about 30 minutes). Drain, reserving ¼ cup liquid. Cover beets with cold water. When cool enough to handle, slip off and discard the skins. Slice beets, and set them aside. Place reserved liquid in saucepan, and stir in vinegar, sugar, and flour. Place over low to medium heat. Cook and stir until thickened, add beets and remaining ingredients, and simmer until heated through.

Boston Baked Beans

Dried beans are an inexpensive way to add nutrition, fiber, and flavor to family meals. They are so popular in Boston that the city is sometimes called "Beantown."

Ingredients:

2 cups dried navy beans or pea beans
½ cup molasses
½ teaspoon dry mustard
¼ teaspoon paprika
1 teaspoon grated onion
1 tablespoon sugar
¾ pound salt pork
salt to taste

Cooking utensils you'll need:
measuring cups
measuring spoons
Dutch oven
small bowl

Directions:

Wash beans and remove any small stones or other debris. Place in Dutch oven, add 4 cups cold water, and soak overnight. The next day, drain the beans reserving the liquid, add 4 cups fresh cold water to beans, bring to a boil over medium heat, cover, lower heat, and *simmer* 1 hour. Meanwhile, mix together the molasses, dry mustard, paprika, onion, salt, and ½ cup reserved water. Preheat oven to 300° Fahrenheit. Drain beans, reserving the water. Stir the molasses mixture into the beans. Wash the salt pork, cut it into 2 pieces, *score* each of them, and bury them in the beans. Cover and bake for 5 hours. Once each hour, remove beans from oven and stir in enough reserved water to keep beans just covered with liquid. After the beans have baked for 5 hours, remove the cover, and bake an additional hour.

New England Food History

The navy bean isn't only the official state vegetable of Massachusetts; it is also the official bean of Boston Baked Beans. The Massachusetts State Legislature granted it this status in 1993.

American Indians were eating beans long before they became a popular food with colonists. Some historians think the Penobscot, Iroquois, and Narragansett people were among the first to make baked beans. Native recipes may have included bear fat and maple syrup. Clay pots that could be buried in hot rocks were used to cook the beans.

The Pilgrims probably substituted pork for the bear fat and molasses for the maple syrup. The fact that one could just mix beans and other ingredients in a pot and then allow them to cook for several hours made baked beans especially popular for cooking on the Sabbath. Sunday was a day of rest, and the Pilgrims were not allowed to spend much time preparing food on this day.

New England Food History

The area from Providence, Rhode Island, to Boston, Massachusetts, is home to many Portuguese immigrants who participated in the whaling and the fishing industries. Large numbers of Portuguese people also settled on Martha's Vineyard and Nantucket Islands.

Although the Portuguese immigrants enjoyed the plentiful seafood available in New England, many early colonists were reluctant to eat clams, originally called "cockles" by some English explorers. Before 1875, they were mostly used as bait for other fish. American Indians may have been the ones who taught settlers in Rhode Island to bake clams by steaming them over hot rocks in a pit. Corn and potatoes could be placed in the pit along with the clams, creating a delicious meal.

Portuguese Steamed Clams

Ingredients:

3 tablespoons olive oil
2 ounces boiled ham, **minced**
¼ cup minced shallots
2 garlic cloves
½ teaspoon dried red pepper flakes (optional)
½ cup cooking wine
½ red bell pepper, minced
18 small, hard–shelled clams
1 tablespoon plus 2 teaspoons lemon juice
½ cup finely chopped fresh coriander leaves

Cooking utensils you'll need:
measuring cups
measuring spoons
large kettle
garlic press (optional)
slotted spoon

Directions:

Wash clams well, and set them aside. Put oil in kettle, and add ham and shallots. Use the garlic press to press the garlic over the ham and shallot mixture. (If you do not have a garlic press, mince the garlic.) Stir in red pepper flakes, place over medium heat, and cook and stir until shallots are tender (about 3 minutes). Add wine, bell pepper, and clams. Cover and steam until clams begin to open (about 5 minutes). As the clams open, use the slotted spoon to transfer them to a serving bowl. Any clams that are not open within 15 minutes should be discarded. Stir lemon juice and coriander into remaining broth, pour over clams, and serve.

Tip:

Alcohol evaporates from wine when it is boiled, leaving the flavor behind.

Lobster Pie for One

Double, triple, or quadruple the ingredients to serve two, three, or four people. Add a salad and your meal is complete.

Ingredients:

7 tablespoons butter
¼ cup cooking sherry
1 tablespoon lemon juice
1 cup cooked lobster
1 tablespoon flour
¾ cup light cream
2 egg yolks

Topping:

¼ cup cracker crumbs
1 tablespoon crushed potato chips
¼ teaspoon paprika
1½ teaspoons Parmesan cheese

Directions:

Using a small amount of butter, grease the pie plate, and set it aside. Place 2 tablespoons of the butter in the saucepan, add sherry, place over medium heat, boil 1 minute, add cooked lobster, remove from heat, and set aside. Melt 3 tablespoons butter in the top of the double boiler by placing that part of the pan over direct medium heat. Add flour, cook and stir for 1 minute, and remove from heat. Drain lobster, adding the liquid to the butter/flour mixture. Stir in the light cream, return to direct heat, cook until thick, stirring constantly, and remove from heat. Preheat oven to 300° Fahrenheit. Place water in the bottom of the double boiler, and put the pan over medium heat. *Whisk* egg yolks in the bowl. Add about ¼ cup of the sauce to the egg yolks, 1 tablespoon at a time, while whisking constantly. Then stir the egg yolk mixture into the remaining sauce. Place the top of the double boiler over the hot water in the bottom of the boiler, and cook for about 3 minutes. Remove the top of the double boiler from the heat source, gently stir in lobster, and pour mixture into the prepared pie plate. Melt the remaining butter, mix it with the topping ingredients, sprinkle on pie, bake for 10 to 15 minutes, and serve.

Tips:

To make cracker crumbs neatly, place crackers in a heavy-duty plastic bag, and crush them with a rolling pin.

Alcohol evaporates from sherry when it is boiled, leaving the flavor behind.

New England Food History

In colonial times, lobster wasn't considered the food delicacy that it is today. In fact, at one time this delicious food was cooked mostly only for servants, prisoners, and children. A group of servants in Massachusetts became so tired of eating the food that they demanded to not be forced to eat lobster more than three times per week.

Maine Lobster Rolls

Maine's coastal waters provide the perfect habitat for this crustacean, helping to make Maine the top producer of lobsters in the United States. These fancy open-faced sandwiches are great for a party or to make any lunch special.

Ingredients:

4 top-sliced hot-dog buns
2 tablespoons butter, softened
3 tablespoons mayonnaise
2 tablespoons **minced** celery
2 cups coarsely chopped cooked cooled lobster

Cooking utensils you'll need:
measuring cup
measuring spoon
small bowl
griddle or heavy skillet

Directions:

Preheat griddle or skillet, spread butter over all sides of buns, and toast buns on griddle or skillet, turning the buns to lightly brown all sides. Mix mayonnaise with celery. Place an equal amount of lobster on each bun, top with mayonnaise mixture, and serve.

Tip:

Both lobster and shrimp can be cooked any way you desire—boiled, grilled, or even in the microwave.

New England History

Until 1820, Maine was actually part of Massachusetts, one of the thirteen original colonies. That's when people living in Maine voted to make it the twenty-third state. Thousands of acres of evergreen forests have encouraged people to nickname it the "Pine Tree State."

The earliest residents of Maine were Abanaki Indians (also called Wabanakis), who engaged in both farming and fishing, and Micmac Indians. The first European settlement occurred in 1607 at Popham; however, the colony could not survive the harsh Maine winters.

New England History

The "granite state," New Hampshire, gets its nickname from the rock that forms its base. Its real name comes from Hampshire, England, the home of John Mason, one of New Hampshire's first colonial residents. The ideals of independence were so strong among the first settlers in New Hampshire that they created an independent republic before the Declaration of Independence was signed in North America.

New England Pot Roast

Cooking utensils you'll need:
measuring cups
measuring spoons
crockpot
saucepan

Preheat oven to 425 degrees Fahrenheit.

Ingredients:

3–pound chuck roast
½ teaspoon salt
¼ teaspoon pepper
2 onions, quartered
1 celery stalk, cut into 8 chunks
4 carrots, quartered
2 teaspoons vinegar
1 bay leaf
1 small cabbage, cut into wedges

Sauce:

3 tablespoons butter
2 tablespoons flour
1 tablespoon instant minced onion
1½ cups beef broth (from crockpot)
1 tablespoon prepared horseradish
½ teaspoon salt

Directions:

Place the onions, celery, and carrots in the crockpot. Wash meat, pat it dry with paper towels, sprinkle all sides with salt and pepper, place it on top of vegetable mixture. Pour 5 cups water over meat. Add vinegar and bay leaf, cover, and cook on low for 5 to 7 hours. Increase heat to high, remove meat and bay leaf, add cabbage, cover, and continue cooking until cabbage is tender (about 15 minutes). Melt butter in saucepan over medium heat, stir in flour, and cook, stirring constantly, until flour is lightly browned. Add remaining sauce ingredients, and cook, stirring as necessary, until thickened. Place roast and vegetables on serving dish and pour sauce over, or serve sauce separately.

New England Boiled Dinner

One-pot meals have been popular since food was cooked over an open fire. This recipe has remained much the same over the years.

Ingredients:

4 pounds corned beef
1 bay leaf
15 peppercorns
8 whole cloves
8 small beets
8 small, whole white onions
2 turnips, diced
16 small, whole new potatoes
16 baby carrots
1 cabbage, cut into 8 wedges

Cooking utensils you'll need:
vegetable scrub brush
stockpot
saucepan

Directions:

Wash meat, pat it dry with paper towels, put it in the stock pot, and add enough water to cover meat. Bring to boil over high heat, cover, lower heat, *simmer* 10 minutes, and remove and discard any scum that forms on top. Add bay leaf, peppercorns, and cloves, cover, and cook until meat is tender (about 3 hours). Meanwhile, scrub beets well, put them in saucepan, cover with water, bring to boil over medium heat, and simmer until tender (about 25 minutes). While beets are cooking, add onions, turnips, potatoes, and carrots to stockpot, cover, and cook an additional 15 minutes. Add cabbage wedges to stockpot, and continue cooking an additional 15 minutes. Meanwhile, drain, and cover beets with cold water. When cool enough to handle, slip off and discard the skins. Place meat on serving platter and slice. Place vegetables around meat and serve.

New England Food History

Boiled Dinner is most likely the modern version of an Old English meal. At one time beef cured with salt was probably used instead of the corned beef that is currently available at most supermarkets. The cloves, bay leaf, and peppercorns used in this recipe are about as exotic as traditional New England food usually gets. Meat was often simply boiled or baked, and the strongly religious colonists of early New England may have considered too many herbs and spices to be a sinful indulgence.

New England Food History

So popular were cranberries among early settlers that a law was passed to regulate picking times. Apparently, some families were a bit too eager and picked cranberries before they were fully ripe. This must have been upsetting to families who were waiting for the berries to ripen before picking, as many berries would be gone before their opportunity to collect them arose. In 1773, Cape Cod passed an ordinance that fined anyone caught picking cranberries before a specified date.

Cranberry Compote

Ingredients:

½ pound fresh cranberries
1 tablespoon grated orange zest
1 teaspoon grated lemon zest
¼ cup orange juice
3 tablespoons lemon juice
½ cup sugar
1 teaspoon vanilla
2 cups water
3 tablespoons cornstarch

Cooking utensils you'll need:
measuring cups
measuring spoons
grater
saucepan
small bowl

Directions:

Place cranberries, fruit zests, fruit juices, sugar, and vanilla in the saucepan. Stir in 1½ cups of the water, bring to boil over medium/high heat, and cook 8 minutes. Mix cornstarch with remaining ½ cup water, and stir into fruit mixture. Reduce heat and *simmer*, stirring constantly, until thickened.

New England Food History

The English settlers who arrived in the New World had a history of making delicious puddings, including Hasty Pudding, one of the most famous. This pudding was stirred on top of the range and is probably the "ancestor" of Indian Pudding. American Indians introduced colonists to cornmeal, which was sometimes called Indian meal by the Europeans. This may be the origin of the name "Indian pudding." Resourceful English cooks gave this name to their pudding when they began using cornmeal as a substitute for the flour they originally used in the dish. American Indians also made a type of cornmeal pudding or porridge they called samp, but it did not include dairy products or molasses.

Indian Pudding

Preheat oven to 300° Fahrenheit.

Ingredients:

4 cups milk
⅓ cup cornmeal
½ cup molasses (or ¼ cup molasses and ¼ cup dark corn syrup)
1 teaspoon grated fresh ginger (or lemon zest)
1 teaspoon salt
1 tablespoon butter
½ pint heavy cream (whipping cream)
1 tablespoon confectioners' sugar (powdered sugar)

Cooking utensils you'll need:
measuring cups
measuring spoons
saucepan
wire whisk
baking dish
electric mixer

Directions:

Use butter to grease baking dish, and set it aside. Place milk in saucepan. Begin to *whisk* milk while slowly adding cornmeal. Place pan over medium heat, and simmer, stirring occasionally, for 20 minutes. Briskly stir in molasses, ginger, salt, and butter. When butter has melted, pour mixture into prepared baking dish, and bake until *set* (about 1½ to 2 hours). Whip cream with confectioners' sugar, and top each serving of pudding with a dollop of cream. Another alternative is to simply pour a small amount of cream over each serving.

Tip:

To whip cream faster, cool beaters in the refrigerator before use.

Maine Wild Blueberry Pie

Preheat oven to 400° Fahrenheit.

Ingredients:

crust:
2 cups plus 3 tablespoons flour
1 teaspoon salt
⅔ cup shortening
⅓ plus 1 tablespoon cold water
1 egg yolk mixed with 1 tablespoon water

filling:
3 tablespoons flour
½ cup sugar (add a little more if a sweeter pie is desired)
5 cups blueberries, washed and drained
½ teaspoon lemon juice
1½ tablespoons butter

Cooking utensils you'll need:
measuring cups
measuring spoons
large mixing bowl
2 small bowls
pastry blender (optional)
rolling pin
bread board or other flat surface
9-inch pie plate
pastry brush

Directions:

For the crust: Mix flour and salt together and *cut* in shortening. Cut in water, divide dough in half, and form each half into a ball. Sprinkle flour on rolling pin and breadboard and roll one dough ball to fit pie plate. (Roll from the center of the dough toward the edge, working your way in all directions. Sprinkle additional flour on rolling pin and lift edges of dough to place additional flour under it if necessary.) Fold dough in half, put pie plate next to dough, slide dough into pie plate, open folded dough, and gently smooth dough into the plate. Place second dough ball on floured board.

For the filling: Mix sugar and flour in small bowl and set aside. Place blueberries in the mixing bowl and *toss* with lemon juice, gently toss with sugar mixture, pour in pie plate, and *dot* with butter. Roll out second dough ball, place it on blueberries, and crimp edges of pie together. Poke the top of the pie in several places with a fork, or cut small slits for steam to escape. Brush top of pie with egg/water mixture, and bake for 40 minutes (until nicely browned).

Tip:

Top each serving with a scoop of vanilla ice cream.

Blueberries and Your Health

In colonial times, American Indians used blueberries for many medicinal purposes. Today, the North American Blueberry Council tells us that blueberries have the highest antioxidant level of forty fruits and vegetables tested. (Antioxidants combat cancer.) They are also thought to help fight macular degeneration, a devastating eye disease.

Maine is the top United States producer of blueberries, one of only three commercially grown fruits native to North America. (The other two are cranberries and concord grapes.)

New England Food History

Historians believe the Iroquois were the first to use maple syrup. According to legend, Woksis threw a tomahawk into a maple tree on a late winter or early spring evening. By the next day, sap had begun to rise in the tree. When the tomahawk was removed that morning, the Indian tasted the sap. Noticing the sweet flavor, he asked that the meat for his dinner be boiled in it. The cooking process reduced the sap, concentrating its sweet taste. Thus the tribe was introduced to this important food source and began tapping trees each year.

Clay pots and hollowed out gourds and logs were used for this purpose. Rocks were heated and dropped into containers holding the sap to make steam rise and concentrate the remaining sap into syrup. This food soon became an important source of the American Indian diet. Some historians report that *sinzibnuckwud*, an Indian name for maple sugar, may have composed as much as 12 percent of the diet of some tribes. Early settlers were so impressed with this new food that stories telling how settlers could obtain syrup and sugar from trees in their own backyard were used to help entice more people to leave Europe for the American colonies. During the Civil War, Northerners considered it patriotic to use maple syrup or maple sugar as a substitute for molasses and cane sugar, which were products of the South.

Today, Vermont is the major source of maple syrup in the United States. Abundant sugar maple trees make it the nation's number-one producer of maple syrup.

Maple–Walnut Sundae

Preheat oven to 425 degrees Fahrenheit.

Ingredients:

½ cup maple syrup
¼ cup brown sugar, firmly packed
⅛ teaspoon salt
½ cup heavy cream
½ cup chopped pecans
1 tablespoon butter
vanilla ice cream

Cooking utensils you'll need:
measuring cups
measuring spoons
nut chopper (optional)
saucepan
candy thermometer

Directions:

Stir together maple syrup, brown sugar, salt, and heavy cream in saucepan. Attach candy thermometer to pan, place pan over medium heat, and stir until sugar is dissolved. Stop stirring, cook to 220º, remove from heat, and quickly stir in pecans and butter. Serve warm syrup over vanilla ice cream.

Tip:

If desired, toast pecans lightly in a pan on top of the stove or in the oven before using them in the syrup.

Leftover syrup will last about 1 week in the refrigerator.

Coffee Milkshake

Ingredients:

1 cup brewed instant coffee, cooled
1 cup milk
1 tablespoon light vanilla syrup
3 scoops coffee ice cream
4 ice cubes

Cooking utensils you'll need:
measuring cup
measuring spoon
ice cream scoop
blender

Directions:

Put everything in the blender, cover, hold your hand on the top, blend until thick and smooth, pour into glasses, and enjoy.

Tip:

Substitute chocolate syrup or ½ teaspoon vanilla for the light vanilla syrup, if desired.

New England Food History

Elsie the cow, the famous symbol for the Borden Company, made her debut in 1939, when she traveled from Massachusetts to New York to be featured at the World's Fair. Today, Vermont is home to the famous ice cream produced by Ben & Jerry's.

Further Reading

Breen, Betty and Earl Mills, Sr. (Chief Flying Eagle of the Cape Cod Mashpee Wampanoags). *Cape Cod Wampanoag Cookbook: Wampanoag Indian Recipes, Images & Lore*. Santa Fe, N.M.: Clear Light Publishers, 2001.

Clark, Melissa and Samara Farber Mormar. *The Nantucket Restaurants Cookbook: Menus and Recipes from the Faraway Isle*. New York: Villard Books, 2001.

Dojny, Brooke and Susan Herrmann Loomis. *The New England Clam Shack Cookbook: Favorite Recipes from Clam Shacks, Lobster Pounds & Chowder Houses*. North Adams, Mass.: Storey Publications, 2003.

Dojny, Brooke. *The New England Cookbook: 350 Recipes from Town and Country, Land and Sea, Hearth and Home*. Boston, Mass.: Harvard Common Press, 1999.

Farmer, Fannie Merritt. *1896 Boston Cooking-School Cookbook*. New York: Gramercy, 1997.

MacDonald, Duncan, and Robb Sagendorph. *Old-Time New England Cookbook*. New York: Dover, 1993.

McKee, Gwen and Barbara Moseley, eds. *Best of the Best from New England: Selected Recipes from the Favorite Cookbooks of Rhode Island, Connecticut,*

Massachusetts, Vermont, New Hampshire, and Maine. Brandon, Mo.: Quail Ridge Press, 1994

Rubin, Jerome. *The Cape Cod Cookbook.* Avon, Mass.: Adams Media Corporation, 2002.

Sloat, Caroline, ed. *The Old Sturbridge Village Cookbook, 2nd: Authentic Early American Recipes for the Modern Kitchen.* Guilford, Conn.: The Globe Pequot Press. 1999.

Stern, Jane and Michael. *Durgin-Park Cookbook: Classic Yankee Cooking in the Shadow of Faneuil Hall.* Nashville, Tenn.: Rutledge Hill Press, 2002.

Tudor, Tasha. *The Tasha Tudor Cookbook: Recipes and Reminiscences from Corgi Cottage.* Boston: Little, Brown and Company, 1993.

Wexler, Jean and Louise King. *Martha's Vineyard Cookbook, 3rd: Over 250 Recipes and Lore from a Bountiful Island.* Guilford, Conn.: The Globe Pequot Press, 1999.

For More Information

Apple History and Nutrition
www.vegparadise.com/highestperch39.html

Food Facts and Lore
www.hungrymonster.com/Foodfacts/Food_Facts.cfm

Lobster History with Photos
octopus.gma.org/lobsters/allaboutlobsters/lobsterhistory.html

Maine Folklife Center's "Foodways Research: A Taste of Maine"
www.umaine.edu/folklife/foodways.htm

Milk History
www.idfa.org/facts/milk/miles.cfm

Molasses Act of 1733
www.multied.com/documents/MOLASSES.html

Molasses Flood History
www.snarkout.org/archives/2003/01/15/

New England Cheese Information
www.newenglandcheese.com

State Agricultural Profiles
www.agclassroom.org

State History
www.theus50.com

Publisher's note:
The Web sites listed on or these pages were active at the time of publication. The publisher is not responsible for Web sites that have changed their addresses or discontinued operation since the date of publication. The publisher will review and update the Web sites upon each reprint.

Index

Author:

In addition to writing, Joyce Libal has worked as an editor for a half dozen magazines, including a brief stint as recipe editor at *Vegetarian Gourmet*. Most of her experience as a cook, however, has been gained as the mother of three children and occasional surrogate mother to several children from different countries and cultures. She is an avid gardener and especially enjoys cooking with fresh herbs and vegetables and with the abundant fresh fruit that her husband grows in the family orchard.

Recipe Tester / Food Preparer:

Bonni Phelps owns How Sweet It Is Café in Vestal, New York. Her love of cooking and feeding large crowds comes from her grandmothers on both sides whom also took great pleasure in large family gatherings.

Consultant:

The Culinary Institute of America is considered the world's premier culinary college. It is a private, not-for-profit learning institution, dedicated to providing the world's best culinary education. Its campuses in New York and California provide learning environments that focus on excellence, leadership, professionalism, ethics, and respect for diversity. The institute embodies a passion for food with first-class cooking expertise.

Recipe Contributor:

Patricia Therrien has worked for several years with Harding House Publishing Service as a researcher and recipe consultant—but she has been experimenting with food and recipes for the past thirty years. Her expertise has enriched the lives of friends and family. Patty lives in western New York State with her family and numerous animals, including several horses, cats, and dogs.

Picture Credits

BrandX: p. 50; Corel: cover; PhotoDisc: cover, pp. 9, 17, 23, 33, 68, 69;
Photos.com: cover, pp. 10, 14, 16, 18, 21, 34, 36, 37, 38, 41, 42, 43, 44, 47, 49, 54,
59, 61, 63, 68, 69; Benjamin Stewart: pp. 13, 14, 16, 25, 26, 31, 53, 56, 69